21st Century
Junior Library

HOW TO BE A DISABILITY ADVOCATE AND ALLY

Nicole Evans and
Tiernan Bertrand-Essington

easterseals

Understanding Disability

Published in the United States of America by:

CHERRY LAKE PRESS
2395 South Huron Parkway, Suite 200, Ann Arbor, Michigan 48104
www.cherrylakepress.com

Reading Adviser: Beth Walker Gambro, MS, Ed., Reading Consultant, Yorkville, IL

Photo Credits: © Rawpixel.com/Shutterstock.com, cover, 1, 15; © Goldsithney/Shutterstock.com, 5;
© Uladzimir Ogonek/Shutterstock.com, 6; © santima.studio/Shutterstock.com, 7; © BAZA Production/
Shutterstock.com, 8, 9; © Ily Andriyanov/Shutterstock.com, 10; © Daisy Daisy/Shutterstock.com, 11;
© Eleonora_os/Shutterstock.com, 12; © wavebreakmedia/Shutterstock.com, 17; © Lopolo/Shutterstock.com, 18;
© Denis Kuvaev/Shutterstock.com, 20

Cherry Lake Press is an imprint of Cherry Lake Publishing Group.

Library of Congress Cataloging-in-Publication Data
Names: Evans, Nicole (Nicole Lynn), author. | Bertrand-Essington, Tiernan, author.
Title: How to be a disability advocate and ally / by Nicole Evans and Tiernan Bertrand-Essington.
Description: Ann Arbor, Michigan : Cherry Lake Publishing, [2022] | Series: Understanding disability |
    Includes bibliographical references. | Audience: Grades 2-3
Identifiers: LCCN 2022005327 | ISBN 9781668909140 (hardcover) | ISBN 9781668910740 (paperback) |
    ISBN 9781668912331 (ebook) | ISBN 9781668913925 (pdf)
Subjects: LCSH: People with disabilities—Political activity—Juvenile literature. | People with disabilities—
    Civil rights—Juvenile literature. | Discrimination against people with disabilities—Juvenile literature.
Classification: LCC HV1568 .E9358 2022 | DDC 362.4—dc23/eng/20220211
LC record available at https://lccn.loc.gov/2022005327

Cherry Lake Press would like to acknowledge the work of the Partnership for 21st Century Learning, a Network
of Battelle for Kids. Please visit http://www.battelleforkids.org/networks/p21 for more information.

Printed in the United States of America
Corporate Graphics

Easterseals is enriching education through greater disability equity, inclusion and access. Join us at www.Easterseals.com.

CONTENTS

What Is a Disability Ally?   4

What Is Ableism?   8

How to Make Positive Change   13

The Importance of
Self-Advocacy   16

Extend Your Learning   21
Glossary   22
Find Out More   23
Index   24
About the Author   24

WHAT IS A DISABILITY ALLY?

One in four people in the United States has a disability. Even though people with disabilities make up so much of the population, they still have difficulty with **inclusion** and equal **opportunity** in many areas of their everyday lives. At school, this could be in the classroom, in the library, in the lunchroom, or on the playground. Also, many places are still not **accessible** to people with disabilities.

Think about a time when someone stood up for you.

5

One of the most powerful things you can do for the disabled community is to become an **ally**. An ally is someone who actively supports and defends the rights

Being an ally is powerful!

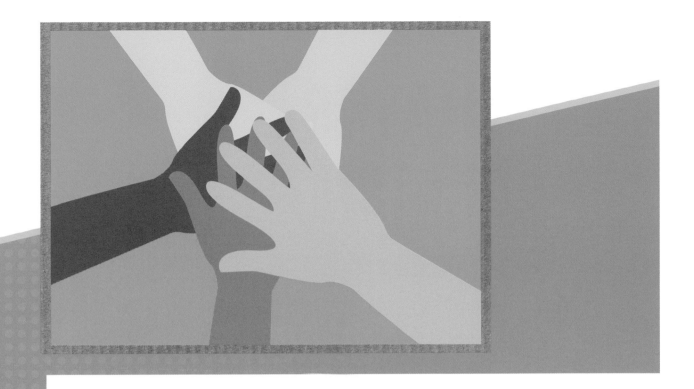

of a group of people that is treated unfairly. An ally is like a friend who sticks up for you! An ally works with you to fight for your rights and equal treatment.

Think!

Of which groups of people do you think you are an ally? The more allies we have, the stronger we are!

WHAT IS ABLEISM?

Discrimination against people with disabilities is called ableism. Ableism is when people with disabilities are treated unfairly.

Ableism can be a person making fun of someone because of their disability. Another example is not letting someone

Think!

Think about all the identities you and your friends have. What are your favorite parts about being you? What do you like about your friends?

9

with a disability participate in a game. Ableism can also be a harmful and untrue attitude that someone has about people with disabilities. We call these things **stereotypes** and **stigmas**. This is not okay! People with disabilities deserve respect and fair treatment just like anybody else.

Look!

Have you ever witnessed ableism in your life?

This is where you come in! Recognizing ableism is the first step to becoming an ally to the disabled community. You may not recognize it until you know what to look for. So educate yourself and others!

Think of ways you can make positive change to help a person with a disability.

HOW TO MAKE POSITIVE CHANGE

The most powerful step you can take toward positive change is to educate yourself about disability issues. And guess what? You are doing just that by reading this book!

It is important to challenge or stop ableism as it happens. This means stepping in, speaking out, and educating others. For example, you may see someone with a disability being bullied.

That's your chance to "ally up" by using your actions and words to end the bullying.

"Allying up" also means correcting someone when they say something mean or incorrect about people with disabilities. For example, if a friend says something mean about people with disabilities, feel confident to speak up. Let your friend know what they said was wrong and hurtful.

Do your best to tell people *why* what they said was wrong or hurtful. Don't worry—you do not have to know everything about disability-related issues to speak up. The important thing is that you

Make a Guess!

If someone says something mean, hurtful, or incorrect about the disabled community, what might you say to correct them?

do your best and remember that you are an ally to the disabled community.

The best way to end ableism is by respecting others and being an ally to your disabled friends. When we respect one another, we can learn what makes each of us special and **unique**.

You can be an ally for the disabled community.

THE IMPORTANCE OF SELF-ADVOCACY

Speaking up for yourself and telling the world what you need and want is called **self-advocacy**. Self-advocacy is an important part of creating change. It brings a voice to a problem that might not be clear to others.

For example, if you use a **mobility device** like a wheelchair, you might be unable to access a part of your school's campus. In that case, it is very important that you speak up and tell teachers, friends, your parents, and school administrators that it is not accessible to you.

When I graduated middle school, there was no ramp or wheelchair access to get onto our school's stage to accept my diploma like everyone else. When my parents found out, they took immediate action! My parents worked with the school administration. They made sure that all graduation stages in our city were accessible to students with disabilities.

This was an important moment in my life because I learned the importance of self-advocacy.

I learned that my voice had **value** and could help me improve my life. My parents were allies to the disabled community. They took action to help solve this problem for me and other students with disabilities.

Speaking up for yourself might sound scary at first, but it is one of the bravest things you can do! When you speak up for yourself, you are creating change

Create!

Self-advocacy requires action! Is there something that you need to speak up about that is affecting you? Write a description of the problem. Then write three possible solutions about how to solve it. Do not wait! Speak up! Get to work! Use your voice to talk to people who can help you solve the problem.

for yourself. However, you are also creating change for other people who are having the same problem. If you ever get nervous about speaking up for yourself, just remember that your words will help others.

Make sure to always listen when someone shares how they feel.

As allies, we can give the spotlight to our friends and peers with disabilities. This might involve using any position of **privilege** we have to raise the voices of people with disabilities. We can make sure their **perspectives** are heard and their needs are met in the spaces we share.

How can you give the spotlight to the disabled community? Is there a situation at school where you have not heard from the perspective of someone who is disabled? Make sure people with disabilities get the chance to speak up!

GLOSSARY

ableism (AY-buh-lih-zuhm) the unfair treatment of people with disabilities

accessible (ik-SEH-suh-buhl) easy to get to or to participate in

ally (AH-lye) a person or group that provides assistance and support

discrimination (dih-skrih-muh-NAY-shuhn) treating someone unfairly because they belong to a particular group or category of people

inclusion (in-KLOO-zhuhn) the act of having everyone participate

mobility device (moh-BIH-luh-tee dih-VYS) equipment designed to help people with disabilities move, including wheelchairs, walkers, canes, and crutches

opportunity (aa-puhr-TOO-nuh-tee) the chance to do or achieve something

perspectives (puhr-SPEK-tivz) the ways things are seen from particular points of view

privilege (PRIV-lij) unearned and sometimes unnoticed advantages

self-advocacy (SELF-AD-vuh-kuh-see) to speak up for yourself and say what you need and want

stereotypes (STEHR-ee-uh-typs) descriptions of people that are oversimplified, incorrect, and insulting

stigmas (STIG-muhs) long-held and incorrect beliefs about someone or something

unique (yoo-NEEK) the only one of its type

value (VAL-yoo) worth and importance

FIND OUT MORE

Books

Bell, Cece. *El Deafo.* New York, NY: Amulet Books, 2020.

Wong, Alice, ed. *Disability Visibility: First-Person Stories from the Twenty-first Century.* New York, NY: Vintage Books, 2020.

Websites

Get Involved with Easterseals
https://www.easterseals.com/get-involved
Learn about the different ways you can get involved in increasing opportunities for people with disabilities, from advocacy to volunteering.

YouTube—Wendy Lu is a Proud Disabled Woman
https://youtu.be/k2MCGqhDepY
Journalist Wendy Wu uses her voice to advocate for people with disabilities.

YouTube—What is the ADA?
https://www.youtube.com/watch?v=zKyjshcxbI0
Check out this cool video to learn more about the ADA!

INDEX

ableism, 8–11, 13–15
accessibility and inclusion
   advocacy needs, 4, 10–11
   self-advocacy, 16–21
advocates and allies
   behavior examples,
      13–14, 21
   combatting ableism,
      8–11, 13–14
   defining, and importance,
      5–7
   self-advocacy, 16–21

bullying, 8, 10, 13–14

discrimination, 8–11, 13–15

education, 11, 13–14

friendships, 5–6, 9

identity, 9

listening, 20–21

privilege, 21

respect, 10, 15

self-advocacy, 16–21
speaking up and speaking out
   by allies, 13–15, 21
   self-advocacy, 16–21
stereotypes, 10

ABOUT THE AUTHORS

Nicole Evans is an actress, writer, and disability rights and inclusion activist. Born with osteogenesis imperfecta, Nicole is a full-time wheelchair user. She enjoys helping children with disabilities explore their identity and realize their full potential. Nicole lives in Los Angeles, California.

Tiernan Bertrand-Essington is a writer and content creator at Change for Balance. Tiernan is a strong ally to the disabled community! He lives in Los Angeles, California.